How Are Insects Helpful?

Molly Aloian

Crabtree Publishing Company

www.crabtreebooks.com

Author
Molly Aloian

Publishing plan research and development
Reagan Miller, Crabtree Publishing Company

Editorial director
Kathy Middleton

Editor
Crystal Sikkens

Proofreader
Kelley McNiven

Indexer
Wendy Scavuzzo

Design
Samara Parent

Photo research
Samara Parent, Crystal Sikkens

**Production coordinator
and prepress technician**
Samara Parent

Print coordinator
Margaret Amy Salter

Photographs
BrandXPictures: pages 6 (moth), 14 (top)
Thinkstock: pages 5 (bottom), 8, 22 (girl and ladybug)
Wikimedia Commons: ForestWander: cover (bottom right);
    Jack Dykinga/USDA: page 10
All other images by Shutterstock

Library and Archives Canada Cataloguing in Publication

Aloian, Molly, author
       How are insects helpful? / Molly Aloian.

(Insects close-up)
Includes index.
Issued in and electronic formats.
ISBN 978-0-7787-1269-5 (bound).--ISBN 978-0-7787-1281-7 (pbk.).--
ISBN 978-1-4271-9363-6 (pdf).--ISBN 978-1-4271-8959-2 (html)

       1. Insects--Juvenile literature. 2. Edible insects--Juvenile
literature. 3. Insects--Ecology--Juvenile literature. I. Title.

QL467.2.A56 2013   j595.7   C2013-904035-8
                                          C2013-904036-6

Library of Congress Cataloging-in-Publication Data

Aloian, Molly.
  How are insects helpful? / Molly Aloian.
       p. cm. -- (Insects close-up)
  Includes Index.
  ISBN 978-0-7787-1269-5 (reinforced library binding) -- ISBN 978-0-7787-
1281-7 (pbk.) -- ISBN 978-1-4271-9363-6 (electronic pdf) -- ISBN 978-1-4271-
8959-2 (electronic html)
  1. Beneficial insects--Juvenile literature. I. Title. II. Series: Aloian, Molly.
Insects close-up.

  SF517.A56 2013
  595.7--dc23
                                    2013023436

Crabtree Publishing Company

www.crabtreebooks.com   1-800-387-7650

Printed in Hong Kong/092013/BK20130703

**Published in Canada
Crabtree Publishing**
616 Welland Ave.
St. Catharines, Ontario
L2M 5V6

**Published in the United States
Crabtree Publishing**
PMB 59051
350 Fifth Avenue, 59th Floor
New York, New York 10118

**Published in the United Kingdom
Crabtree Publishing**
Maritime House
Basin Road North, Hove
BN41 1WR

**Published in Australia
Crabtree Publishing**
3 Charles Street
Coburg North
VIC 3058

Contents

What is an insect?

An insect is a kind of animal called an **invertebrate**. An invertebrate is an animal that does not have a **backbone**. Insects belong to a big group of invertebrates called **arthropods**.

All insects have six legs and three main body sections. Many insects also have wings.

What do you think?

The wasp on the right is an insect. How can you tell?

4

Awesome armor

Instead of a backbone, an insect has a hard covering over its body called an **exoskeleton**. An exoskeleton protects the insect's body and helps to keep it dry.

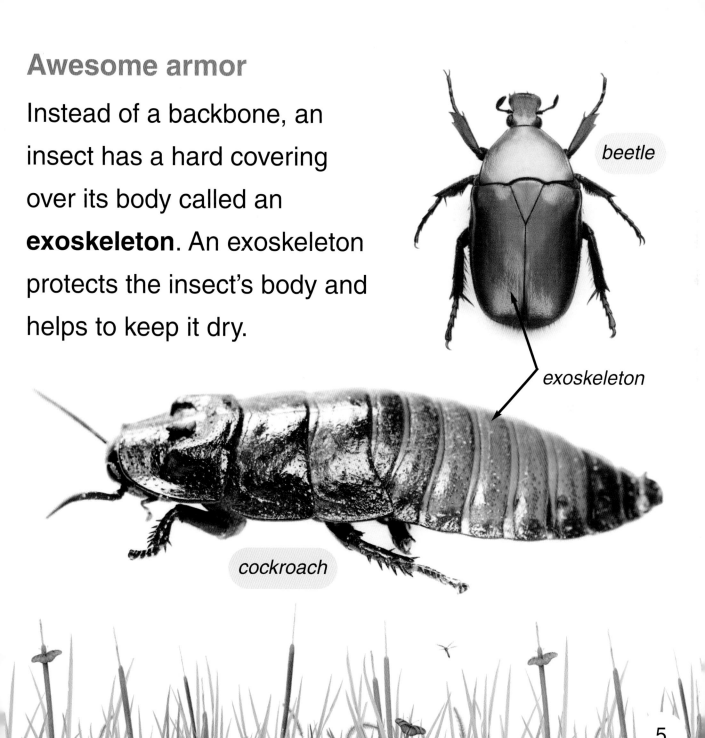

beetle

exoskeleton

cockroach

Insects are important

Insects are important to many living things. Insects help plants, animals, and people. Insects are food for many other animals, and even some plants! Without insects, these animals and plants would not be able to survive.

The Venus flytrap is a kind of plant that eats insects.

We need insects

Many plants also need insects
to help them make seeds. Seeds
grow into new plants. Insects provide
people with items such as honey and
silk. Keep reading to find out other ways
insects are important to
the planet.

moth

honeybee

grasshopper

praying mantis

More than half of all the animals on Earth are insects.
Think about how different the world would be without them!

Food for other animals

All animals must eat to stay alive. Insects are food for many other animals. Spiders, scorpions, bats, birds, and frogs are just some of the animals that eat insects. Without insects, these animals would not have enough food to eat.

What do you think?

This bird is called a bee-eater. Can you guess what kind of insect is its favorite food?

Insect-eater

Some animals must eat a lot of insects in order to survive. For example, anteaters eat thousands of ants and termites every day. They search for ants and termites on the ground and in trees.

Anteaters use their long noses to search for ants and termites.

Eating pests

Insects must eat to stay alive, too. Some insects eat plants and others eat animals. Some insects that eat animals help Earth by eating **pests**. Pests can damage plants that animals and people eat.

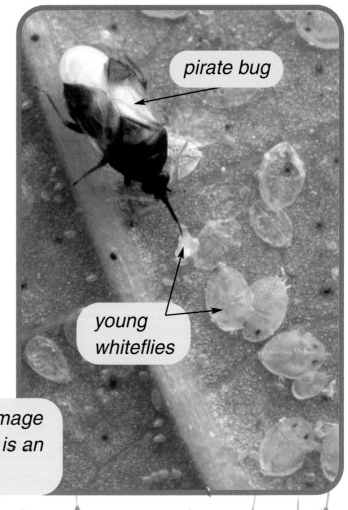

pirate bug

young whiteflies

Whiteflies are pests that can damage vegetable plants. The pirate bug is an insect that eats these pests.

Ladybugs eat aphids

Aphids are tiny insects that kill milkweed plants by sucking juice from the plant's stem. Milkweed is an important food for monarch caterpillars. Ladybugs help to protect this food source by eating the aphids.

milkweed stem

aphid

ladybug

monarch caterpillar

11

Clean-up crews

Other insects, such as flies and beetles, are helpful because they are **scavengers**. Scavengers are animals that eat dead plants and animals. Scavengers help keep natural areas clean and healthy.

These flies are scavengers. They are eating a dead fish.

Dinnertime!

Some scavengers even eat animal waste! Dung beetles are insects that eat animal waste. These insects help keep animal waste from piling up. Too much waste can make other living things sick.

What do you think?

Termites are insects that feed on dead wood. Are they scavengers? Why or why not?

Dung beetles roll animal waste into balls. This makes their food easier to move.

13

Spreading pollen

Some plants need **pollen** from other plants in order to make seeds. Insects such as moths, bees, and butterflies carry pollen from one plant to another. Moving pollen from one plant to another is called **pollination**.

What do you think?

What would be different about Earth if there were no **pollinators**?

moth

pollen

Helping plants grow

Insects eat pollen from flowers. When an insect lands on a flower, some of the pollen rubs off onto its body. This pollen then rubs off the insect onto the next flower it lands on. Flowers that have pollen from other plants can make seeds. New plants grow from the seeds.

Insects pollinate at least 90 different fruit and vegetable plants.

Making honey and beeswax

Honeybees help with pollination, but they also make honey and beeswax inside their bodies. People eat honey, and they use beeswax to make candles, crayons, and other items.

Soap can be made from beeswax.

beeswax candles

honey

Sweet honey

Honeybees collect **nectar** from flowers. They bring the nectar back to their **hives** where it is turned into honey and stored for food. The honey a bee eats is made into beeswax inside the bee's body. Bees use the wax when building their hives.

Beekeepers are people who collect the honey stored in the hives that the bees do not need.

beeswax

honey

Making silk

Silkworm caterpillars are also helpful insects. Silkworm caterpillars make **cocoons** before they turn into moths. The cocoons are made of silk. People use this silk to make material for clothing and other items. Silk is shiny, soft, and strong.

Silkworm cocoons are white or yellow. The silk can later be dyed to make different colors.

Strong silk

Silkworm caterpillars can make about six inches (15 centimeters) of silk in just one minute. People can use the silk to make dresses, pajamas, scarves, ties, and curtains. It takes over one thousand cocoons to collect enough material to make just one silk dress.

silk scarf

silk tie

silk pajamas

Dirt diggers

Some insects, such as ants, are helpful because they dig tunnels through dirt. As they dig, they move deep layers of dirt up to the top of the ground. This helps keep the dirt **fertile**. Dirt that is fertile is full of important **nutrients**.

Anthills are created as ants move dirt from underground to the surface.

Full of nutrients

Nutrients are natural substances that help plants and animals grow and stay healthy. All kinds of plants grow in fertile dirt. Animals and people eat these plants. People also eat the fruits and vegetables that come from many of these plants.

Strawberry plants grow tasty fruit in fertile dirt.

Make a buzz!

This activity will help teach your family and friends how insects are helpful. Choose one or more helpful insects. Make a poster that shows pictures of how these insects are helpful. Write under each picture how the insect helps Earth. Show your poster to your family and friends.

HELPFUL INSECTS

Silkworms make Silk for clothing.

Moths pollinate flowers.

Ladybugs eat pests.

Dung beetles clean up waste.

Bees make honey and beeswax.

Learning more

Books

Feldman, Thea. *Insects in Action* (American Museum of Natural History Readers). Sterling, 2012.

Spilsbury, Louise A. *Caterpillar Capers (Crabtree Connections).* Crabtree Publishing Company, 2011.

Kalman, Bobbie. *The ABCs of Insects* (ABCs of the Natural World) . Crabtree Publishing Company, 2009.

Aloian, Molly and Bobbie Kalman. *Helpful and Harmful Insects* (The World of Insects). Crabtree Publishing, 2005.

Websites

The Centre for Bug Smart Living: Helpful Insects
www.bugsmart.ca/bug/helpful/

Helpful Insects
www.insectidentification.org/helpful_insects.asp

BBC Nature – All Insects
www.bbc.co.uk/nature/life/Insect/by/rank/all

10 Most Important Insects in the World: Discovery Channel
http://dsc.discovery.com/tv-shows/curiosity/topics/10-most-important-insects.htm

Words to know

Note: Some boldfaced words are defined where they appear in the book.

backbone (BAK-bohn) noun A row of bones down the middle of an animal's back

cocoons (kuh-KOONS) noun Special cases made of silk that caterpillars spin around themselves before turning into adult insects

fertile (FUR-tl) adjective Describing land that is able to grow plenty of crops

hives (hahyvs) noun Places where bees and wasps live

nectar (NEK-ter) noun A sweet liquid found in flowers

nutrients (NOO-tree-uhnts) noun Natural substances that help plants and animals grow and stay healthy

pollen (POL-uhn) noun A powdery substance found in flowers that plants need to make seeds

pollinator (POL-uh-nayt-ur) noun An animal that moves pollen between flowers

silk (silk) noun A strong, thin material that certain caterpillars make inside their bodies

A noun is a person, place, or thing. An adjective is a word that tells you what something is like.

Index